Chloe Kim

CHERRY LAKE PRESS

Published in the United States of America by Cherry Lake Publishing
Ann Arbor, Michigan
www.cherrylakepublishing.com

Reading Adviser: Marla Conn, MS, Ed., Literacy specialist, Read-Ability, Inc.
Book Designer: Jennifer Wahi
Illustrator: Jeff Bane

Photo Credits: © Jon Bilous/Shutterstock, 5; © T.Dallas/Shutterstock, 7; © Tom Wang/Shutterstock, 9; © Olya Lytvyn/Shutterstock, 11; © Andrey_Popov/Shutterstock, 13; © Leonard Zhukovsky/Shutterstock, 15, 17, 22, 23; © Helen89/Shutterstock, 19; © Starstock/Dreamstime.com, 21; Cover, 1, 8, 12, 18, Jeff Bane; Various frames throughout, © Shutterstock images

Cherry Lake Press is an imprint of Cherry Lake Publishing Group.

Library of Congress Cataloging-in-Publication Data

Names: Pincus, Meeg, author. | Bane, Jeff, 1957- illustrator.
Title: Chloe Kim / Meeg Pincus ; illustrated by Jeff Bane.
Description: Ann Arbor, Michigan : Cherry Lake Publishing, 2021. | Series: My itty-bitty bio | Includes index. | Audience: Grades K-1
Identifiers: LCCN 2020005534 (print) | LCCN 2020005535 (ebook) | ISBN 9781534168411 (hardcover) | ISBN 9781534170094 (paperback) | ISBN 9781534171930 (pdf) | ISBN 9781534173774 (ebook)
Subjects: LCSH: Kim, Chloe, 2000---Juvenile literature. | Snowboarders--United States--Biography--Juvenile literature. | Olympic athletes--Biography--Juvenile literature.
Classification: LCC GV857.S57 P56 2021 (print) | LCC GV857.S57 (ebook) | DDC 796.93092 [B]--dc23
LC record available at https://lccn.loc.gov/2020005534
LC ebook record available at https://lccn.loc.gov/2020005535

Printed in the United States of America
Corporate Graphics

About the author: Meeg Pincus has been a writer, editor, and educator for 25 years. She loves to write inspiring stories for kids about people, animals, and our planet. She lives near San Diego, California, where she enjoys the beach, reading, singing, and her family.

About the illustrator: Jeff Bane and his two business partners own a studio along the American River in Folsom, California, home of the 1849 Gold Rush. When Jeff's not sketching or illustrating for clients, he's either swimming or kayaking in the river to relax.

I was born in Long Beach, California. It was 2000.

I have two older sisters.

My parents are **immigrants**.
They're from South Korea.

Where is your family from?

My parents **value** education. I went to school in Switzerland for 2 years. It was a good school. But I was bullied for being different. It was hard to make friends at first.

What's good about being different?

I learned to snowboard. I was a **natural**. I entered my first contest. I was 6 years old.

My parents encouraged me to **pursue** my dreams. They **sacrificed** a lot to help me succeed.

I practiced hard. I became a **professional** snowboarder at age 12.

I won an **Olympic** gold medal for snowboarding. I was 17 years old. I was the youngest girl in history to do this.

I started college at Princeton University in 2019. I'm studying science.

What do you like studying?

I love to snowboard. I love to learn. I **encourage** young people to dream big.

What do you want to ask me?

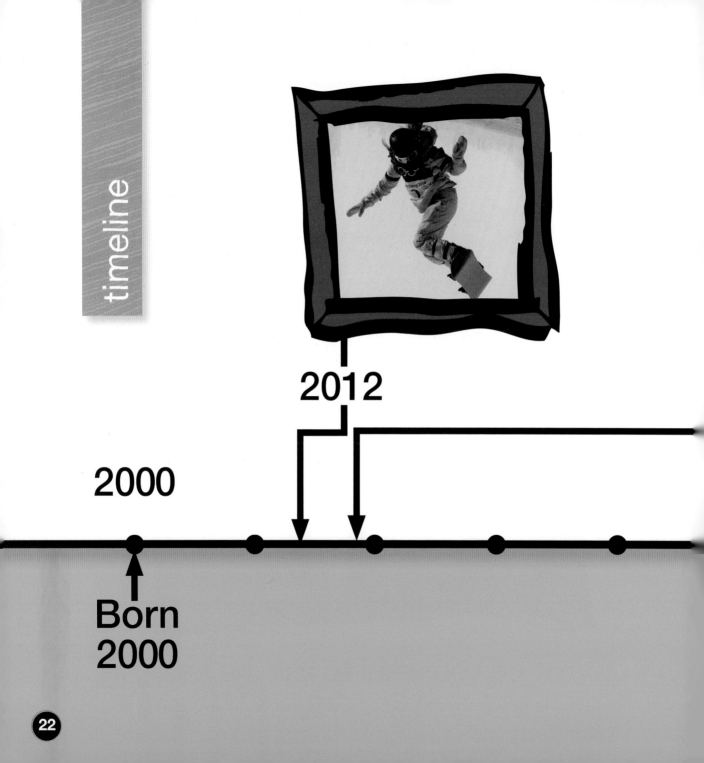

2012

2000

Born
2000

2018

2100

glossary

encourage (en-KUR-ij) to give someone hope that they can do something

immigrants (IM-ih-gruhnts) people who move from one country to another and settle there

natural (NACH-ur-uhl) a person who has special skills or talents

Olympic (uh-LIM-pik) relating to the Olympic Games, which are summer and winter contests for athletes from all over the world

professional (pruh-FESH-uh-nuhl) making money for working hard at something others do for fun

pursue (pur-SOO) to follow

sacrificed (SAK-ruh-fised) gave up something for the sake of something or someone else

value (VAL-yoo) to think that something is very important

index